Contents

Why do we need water? 4

What happens when there is no water? 8

How do people get water in California? 10

How do people get water in Bali? 18

How did people get water in Machu Picchu? 24

How has irrigation been used in different places and times? 30

Glossary 31

Why do we need water?

Water takes many forms. Water is a drop of sweat from our bodies. Water is a cloud, a raindrop, or a snowflake. It is hail, sleet, or ice. Water is a pond, a lake, a stream, a river, or an ocean.

Most of the earth's surface is covered with water, but most of the water is in the oceans. Ocean water is too salty for you to drink. In many places around the world, clean, fresh water can be hard to find.

Water has always been important for human life. Animals and plants also need water to live.

More than half the human body is made up of water. Your body needs water every day. You take in water when you drink water, milk, juice, or other liquids. You also put water into your body when you eat.

In your home, you not only drink water, but you also use it to shower, wash your hands and face, and brush your teeth. You also use it to cook, clean, wash dishes and clothes, and flush the toilet.

Outside your home, you may use water for swimming, boating, fishing, or for simply splashing and cooling off.

Farmer harvesting crops

Water feed pipe at a power plant

People living in big cities and small towns all over the world need water for their own daily use. In addition, factories use water to make products, power plants use it to make electricity, and farms use it to grow crops.

What happens when there is no water?

Where there isn't enough rain to give people the water they need, they must find a way to bring water from other places. Bringing water to a place where it's needed is called **irrigation.**

Irrigation water comes from lakes, springs, rivers, and streams. People dig **canals** in the ground to guide the water to where they need it. The water flows through the canals to farm fields, towns, and cities.

Irrigation can turn the dry land of **deserts** into good farmland. In many places where the weather is mild, irrigation makes it possible for farmers to grow two crops each year.

People have used irrigation for many thousands of years. All around the world, people have built irrigation systems to bring water to their cities, towns, and farms.

How do people get water in California?

California is located on the West Coast of the United States. It is the third largest state. More people live in California than in any other state, and more keep moving there all the time. Today California has some of the best farmland in the world, but it wasn't always that way.

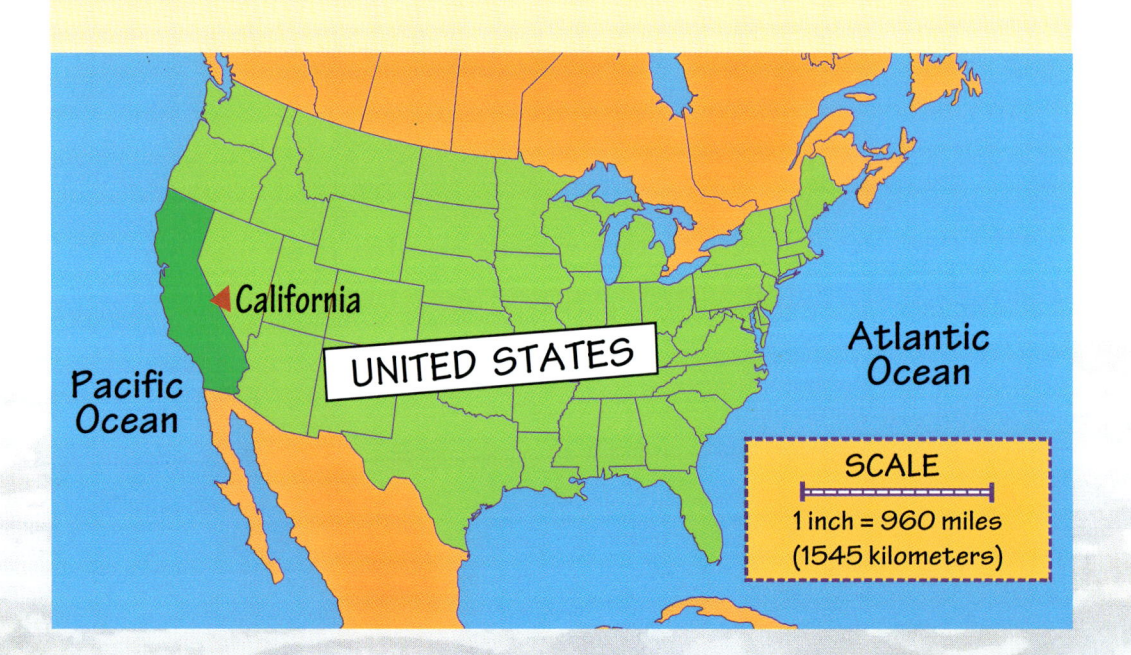

California

Pacific Ocean

UNITED STATES

Atlantic Ocean

SCALE
1 inch = 960 miles
(1545 kilometers)

Redwood forest in northern California

California is a land of contrasts. It has beautiful green forests in the northwest and hot, dry deserts in the south.

The north gets plenty of snow and rain during the winter and spring and, as a result, has plenty of water during these months. In the south, there is little rainfall. Since most of the people live in the south, there is not enough water to meet the needs of the people there.

Death Valley in southern California

State of California

Oroville Dam

Sacramento

Los Angeles

San Diego

To provide water to these people, California's government decided to build a large irrigation system called the State Water Project to bring water from the north to the south.

The State Water Project begins north of Sacramento, at Oroville Dam. The government built this **dam** to create a large pool called a **reservoir.** The reservoir collects water for later use in the south.

Oroville Dam

California Aqueduct

The California Aqueduct is 444 miles long—one of the longest aqueducts in the world. Millions of gallons of water flow through its open canal and huge steel **pipelines.**

The California Aqueduct winds through the western San Joaquin Valley. Here water from the aqueduct has turned dry land into some of the best farmland in the world.

State of California

Delta

Map labels: Sacramento, Delta, Aqueduct, Los Angeles, San Diego — State of California

Below the dam, the water flows downriver to a marsh called the Delta. Here powerful pumps suck the water across the Delta and lift it to the top of a hill. From there, a canal called the California **Aqueduct** takes the water to cities and farms in the south.

Fruits and nuts grown in the San Joaquin Valley are shipped all over the United States. These crops include almonds, apricots, cantaloupes, grapes, kiwi fruit, nectarines, oranges, peaches, pistachios, plums, and walnuts. A lot of these foods have probably ended up on your plate!

State of California

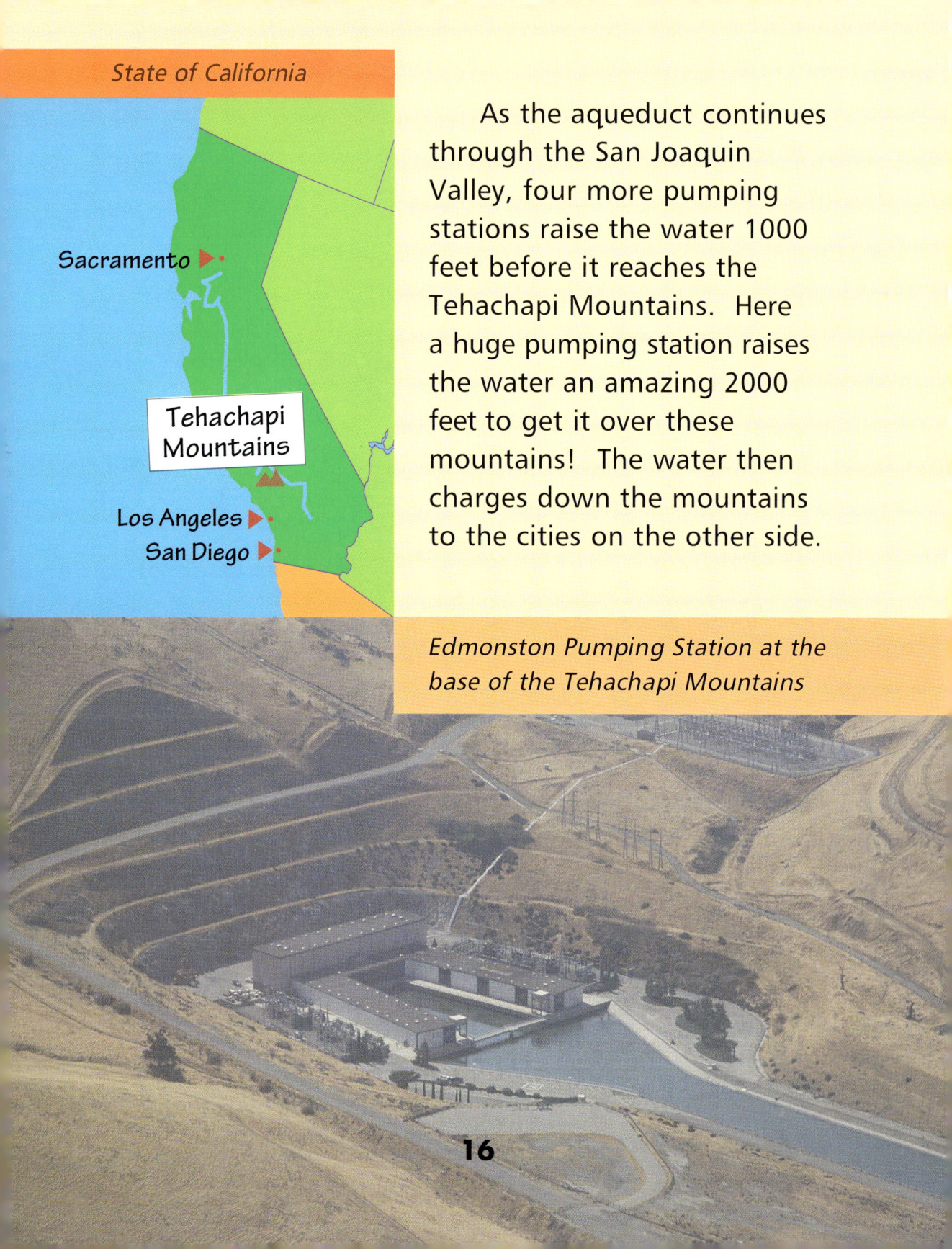

As the aqueduct continues through the San Joaquin Valley, four more pumping stations raise the water 1000 feet before it reaches the Tehachapi Mountains. Here a huge pumping station raises the water an amazing 2000 feet to get it over these mountains! The water then charges down the mountains to the cities on the other side.

Edmonston Pumping Station at the base of the Tehachapi Mountains

The people living in Los Angeles and other cities along the southern coast rely on the California Aqueduct to meet most of their water needs. Without this water, these cities could never have become as large as they are today.

Of course, the larger a city grows, the more water it needs. Los Angeles is the second largest city in the United States—such a large city needs a lot of water! The California Aqueduct is large enough to bring in this huge amount of water.

How do people get water in Bali?

Bali is a small island in the Indian Ocean that lies between Australia and mainland Southeast Asia. It's one of many islands that make up the country of Indonesia. Mountains run the whole length of the island, and some are active volcanoes.

Unlike most of California, Bali receives a lot of rain. However, most of it falls during the rainy season. Farmers need irrigation to make sure that their fields don't receive too much water in the wet season and too little in the dry season.

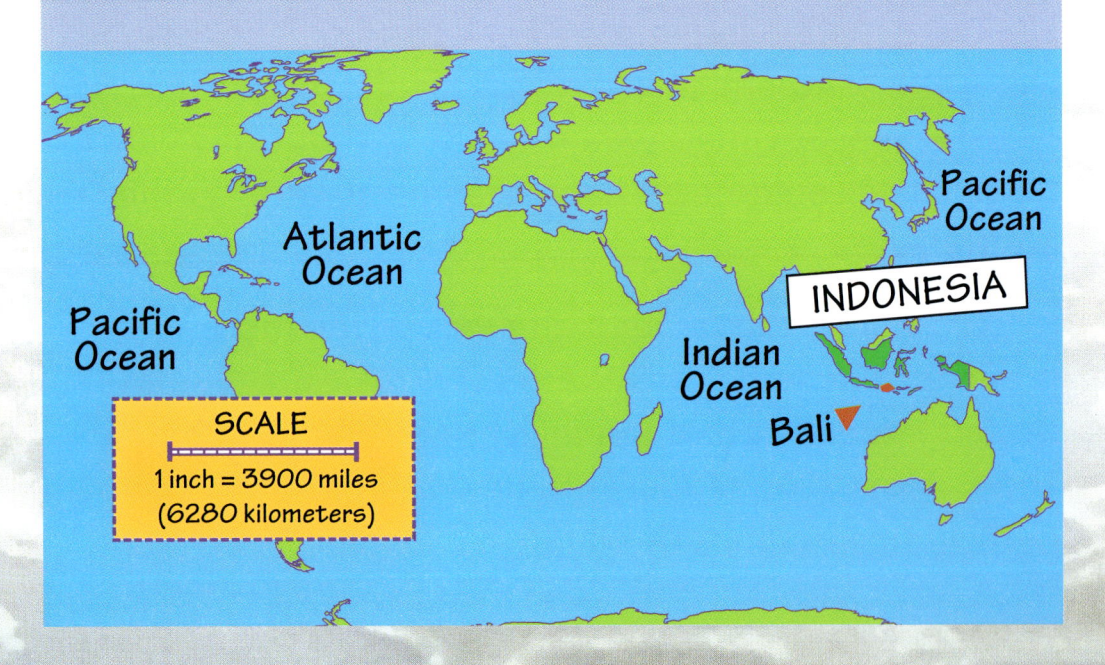

Pacific Ocean
Atlantic Ocean
Pacific Ocean
Indian Ocean
INDONESIA
Bali

SCALE
1 inch = 3900 miles
(6280 kilometers)

For more than a thousand years, the people of Bali have used irrigation systems to bring water to their fields. Many of these systems get water from rivers that flow down the volcanoes. Dams made of logs, earth, and stones force the water to flow into rock-lined **tunnels.** The tunnels take the water to stone canals and bamboo pipes that deliver it to farmers' fields.

Stone canal

Some of the tunnels in use today were built many years ago. To build them, teams of men began working at opposite ends and kept digging until they met. The soft rock of the volcanoes has held these tunnels in place for hundreds of years.

Farmers also built **terraces,** which look like large steps going up the side of a mountain. Each step is a field used for growing rice, vegetables, or coffee. These terrace fields each receive water from the canals and pipes.

Balinese terraces

Balinese farmers belong to religious farming groups called **subaks**. Each field has a subak **shrine** at the spot where irrigation water enters the field. Upstream is a water temple that several subaks share. A priest comes to bless the water before each subak plants and then returns at each stage of their crop's growth.

Subak shrine with offerings

Since many subaks use the same stream for irrigation water, all farm work must be carefully timed. The **religious ceremonies** at the water temple tell subaks when to water, plant, and **harvest** their crops. Directed by these ceremonies, farmers place logs in the irrigation canals to force water to flow to certain fields.

In 1971 the Indonesian government took control of the planting and irrigation schedule from the subaks. The government thought they could control the planting and flow of water better than the subaks.

Under the government's new plan, farmers no longer used the water temples and their ceremonies to time their irrigation. Balinese farmers were confused, and the results were poor.

Balinese water temple

Balinese farmers planting rice

In 1981 the government began returning control of the irrigation to the subaks. It had decided that the traditional way worked better. The subaks once again used the religious ceremonies of their water temples to control irrigation. Today Bali uses the same irrigation system it has used for more than a thousand years.

How did people get water in Machu Picchu?

On a ledge between two peaks in the Andes Mountains stands the old stone city of Machu Picchu. More than five hundred years ago, Machu Picchu was part of a kingdom of Native South Americans known as the **Inca**. Today it is in a country called Peru, on the western side of South America.

During Inca times, Machu Picchu was a religious center where only a small group of people lived. Today no one lives there, but thousands of people from all over the world visit what is left of this city every year.

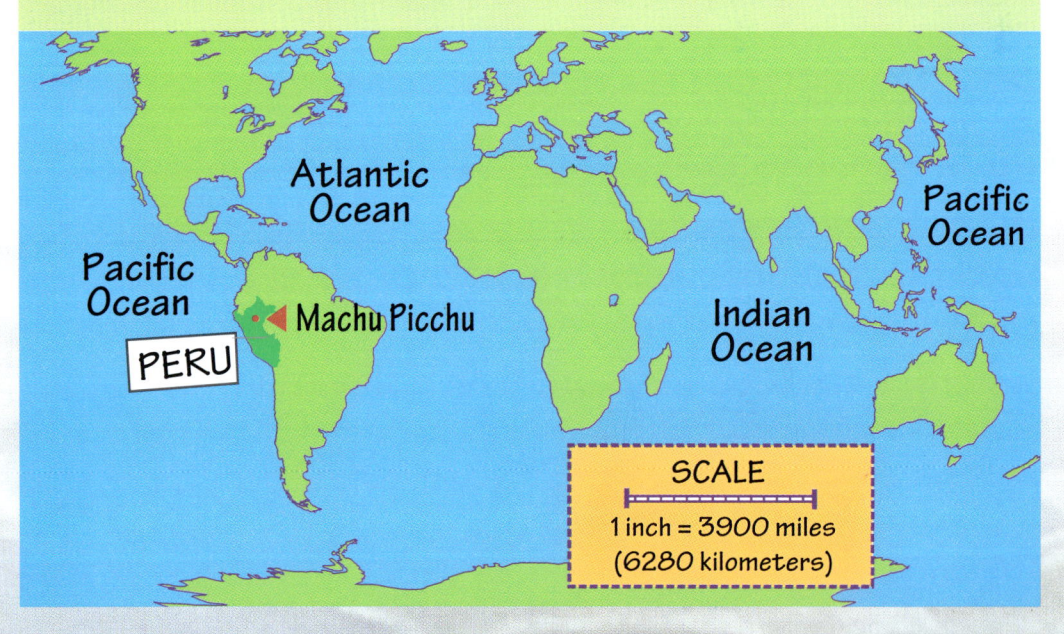

SCALE
1 inch = 3900 miles
(6280 kilometers)

Like the Balinese, Inca farmers needed irrigation water for their crops. They built terraces going up the mountainsides around Machu Picchu. There they grew potatoes, corn, vegetables, and fruits.

The terraces made irrigating the crops easier and kept good soil from washing away.

The people of Machu Picchu got water from nearby mountain springs. They built stone canals to bring the water from these springs to where it was needed. To hold the water for later use, they built stone-lined reservoirs in farmers' fields with their hands.

Mountain spring in the Andes Mountains

Unused canals in Machu Picchu

    The irrigation canals for these terraces came down the mountain's slopes in a winding course. Each terrace was given just enough water to wet it without overflowing the terrace's side. Inca farmers checked the canals year-round to keep them free of dirt and rubble so that the water could flow easily.

The people of Machu Picchu also needed water for their personal use, just like we do today. They used it to wash, clean, and cook.

In addition, the women of this religious center had some special uses for the water. They used it to create dyes for the wool used in making the priests' religious robes. They also used it to make *chicha*, a corn drink for religious ceremonies.

Peruvian woman using a traditional weaving loom

Stairway of the Fountains

    Water from the springs flowed through canals, over stone steps, and into sixteen stone basins in the city. This water system is called the "Stairway of the Fountains." Inca women filled ceramic jugs with this water and carried them to the houses and other buildings for use.

    Because of this unusual irrigation system, Machu Picchu has been called "The City of the Stairs."

How has irrigation been used in different places and times?

Around the world, people have been using irrigation systems to get water for home use and farming for thousands of years. Today the California Aqueduct brings water to many farms and homes. The stone canals of Machu Picchu brought water to the city and its terraces hundreds of years ago. Some of the tunnels and canals of Bali are even older, and they're still being used.

People, animals, and plants need water to live. Irrigation has been helping the world bring water to where it is needed for a very long time. It will continue to help our world in the future.

Glossary

aqueduct big canal that carries a large amount of water 13

canal waterway that carries water long distances, from one place to another 8

dam barrier that stops the flow of water 12

desert hot, dry place with little or no rain 9

harvest to gather farm crops for eating, storing, and selling 21

Inca people who lived in Peru, South America, a long time ago before Europeans came to the Americas 24

irrigation system that brings water to a place where it's needed 8

pipeline long pipe that carries water 14

religious ceremony act that is done at a certain time in connection with a religion (for example: wedding, bar mitzvah) 21

reservoir very large pool built to hold water for later use 12

shrine object or place where people go to pray 21

subak religious farming group in Bali that helps farmers plan when crops are watered, planted, and harvested 21

terrace farming field that looks like a very wide step going up the side of a mountain 20

tunnel passageway under something or through something 19